D0618640

START SELLING:

A GUIDE FOR SURVIVAL AND SUCCESS IN SALES

M. Patrick Campbell

information, content, or strategies. Any and all claims or representations as to income and earnings are not to be considered as "average earnings".

Published by:
The Books Factory
www.TheBooksFactory.com

A portion of the profits of every book supports charities that empower the health and education of women and children.

ISBN: 978-1-950336-00-5

For Ian, Charlotte, Yasmine, and Muffin

TABLE OF CONTENTS

INTRODUCTION

I was seventeen when I first learned how to sell. I needed to learn fast, because my family depended on my success.

My parents had sent my sister and me to private schools, and the school fees ate deeply into their resources. Money was always tight.

I spent the summers with my grandmother. We called her "Muffin" because she liked to eat muffins. Muffin ran a summer cabin rental business in New Hampshire. In the evenings, I worked as a busboy at a Chinese restaurant up the street, and during the day, I helped Muffin out with her cabins.

Frankly, there wasn't much to do for her, as she was pretty passive about sales and the business. If people came and asked to rent a cabin, she let them have one. If no one turned up, she didn't try to change that. I sensed that there might be a way to make more money.

My chance came in 1982, when I was seventeen and Muffin was too frail to manage the cabin rental business any longer. My family put me in charge. I resolved to be proactive and aimed to fill up every night to the best of my ability. With only one employee, my nine-year-old sister Sarah, we got to work and started selling.

I learned how to sell, applied my skills with enthusiasm, and succeeded. Initially, I just wanted to make sure we didn't lose money. But by my second year, the two of us were making a real financial contribution to our family and expanding the business.

Later, I sold customized educational trips to China and private equity funds, and in 2010, I started my own firm to help private fund managers raise institutional capital for their funds. Along the way, I learned a lot.

In this book, I'm going to share with you what I've learned, and I'll show you how you can make those insights work for you.

My father once told me, "If you don't have a plan for yourself, someone else will." This book will help you develop your plan.

In Chapter 1, we'll explore the WHY – why you want to go into sales – and focus on your personal motivation.

Chapters 2, 3 and 4 are all about preparing to sell: WHAT you are selling, WHO you'll sell to, and getting mentally ready. In Chapter 5, you'll take the leap into action.

From Chapter 5 on, you'll get the practical tools you need for success – the HOW. This includes not only practical sales techniques but also how to learn from other people and your own mistakes, how to deal with difficult situations, and how to stay strong when the going gets tough.

Step by step, you'll learn:

- How to approach your new sales job.

- How to make buyers value and trust you.

- Professional techniques for sales conversations.

- How to stay focused both in the short term and over the long haul.

- Managing your emotions in rewarding and challenging times.

At the end, you'll be ready to approach any sales position because you'll have a road map to success.

To avoid clumsy "he or she" and "him or her" sentences, I'll sometimes use male pronouns and sometimes female. Almost everything I say in this book applies to either gender. Whether you're a salesman or a saleswoman, this book is for you.

Are you ready?

Let's go!

CHAPTER 1

WHY DO YOU WANT TO SELL?

In 1991, I was twenty-seven and had borrowed $60,000 to go to business school at the University of Chicago. That was a lot of money for me. I had thought I wanted to become a management consultant, a career that sounded glamorous and important on paper.

But a few months into my MBA program, after listening to many management consultant presentations, I realized this wasn't for me. The final straw for me was a presentation by a senior executive of a prominent consulting firm who extolled the importance of communication skills but was barely able to articulate the simple concepts. If this was a management consultant, I didn't want to become one. Halfway through the presentation, I walked out into a cold Chicago winter night.

Despite the freezing temperature, I broke out into a panicked sweat. What a huge mistake I had made! What had I done?! My head pounded with one question: If I'm not going to be a management consultant, how will I pay off my loan?

The next day, I had rugby practice for our university team. I told some of my teammates about my dilemma. Many were already one year ahead of me in business school and, thus, one year wiser.

"I don't know what to do," I confessed. "How am I going to pay this money back?"

"Sales and trading," three of them said almost simultaneously. They were talking about selling or trading securities on Wall Street. One of them added, "All it takes is one good year, and you'll wipe all that debt away with your bonus."

At the word "sales" my heart leaped with hope. I knew something about how to sell – hadn't I sold cabin rentals for the family business?

True, I knew nothing about banking, securities, or Wall Street. But I would figure out what I was going to sell and who I would sell to.

I started searching. Big banks weren't a good fit for me because I had grown up in small businesses. So, unlike many of my peers, I didn't go through a training program at one of the big investment banks. Instead, I worked for small firms with minimal training and support. The environment was competitive, but I used the skills I had taught myself at a young age and picked up new techniques along the way to first survive and then succeed.

In just three years out of business school, I had such a good bonus that I was debt free.

If you want to be successful in sales, you have to want to sell – really, really want to sell.

WHAT MOTIVATES YOU?

Think about why you chose this path. Identify your motivation, because this is what will keep you going in tough times.

Your motivation may change throughout your career. For example, my initial motivation was to pay off my debt – a financial motivation. Once I had achieved that, my next goal was to be a partner at my firm – a motivation based on status. Sometimes, several motivations drive you at once. That's fine. Just identify what's behind your desire.

Here are some common motivations:

- Make more money. You may seek a higher income either for the sake of the money itself, or for a specific goal, such as to pay off your student loan (like I did), to support your family, to buy a house, or to travel.

- As a career move. Perhaps you simply need a job – any job – and the only vacancies are in sales. Or maybe you want a business-related career and only sales positions are available.

- Ambition and competitiveness. You thrive in a competitive environment where you can measure yourself against rivals, beat everybody, and become Number One. The sales sector is great for comparing results and racing to the front spot.

- Social. You want a job in which you can meet and talk with people.

- Effect a positive change in the buyer's organization.

- Flexible schedule. You want a job in which you can plan your work hours, perhaps to fit around the needs of your family, your studies, or another job.

- Help the company. Perhaps it's your family's business or your own, and the company faces a dire financial situation because nobody else is willing to take on sales. Perhaps the main (or only) salesperson in your company has left, and you need to step in until they hire a replacement.

- Travel. You enjoy driving or visiting different towns or regions. A frequent change of scenery boosts your energy, so you want a job where you don't have to stay cooped up in the same office day after day.

- Work from home. You want a job that allows you to work online or on the phone, so you can keep an eye on your young children, ailing parents, or farm animals.

- Appreciation from your boss and peers. In most enterprises, salespeople are highly valued and prized. Your boss and coworkers know that you're the one who generates the revenue and the money for their salaries.

- Market your own product. You may be an entrepreneur or inventor and have created a new product or service. Only you understand how it works and can explain and sell it.

Take a moment, think about what motivates you, and write that reason down. This will anchor it in your mind.

WHY ARE SALESPEOPLE IMPORTANT?

It all starts with a sale. No revenue, no business. Period.

Look around the businesses in your town or on TV. Although you can buy a lot of things with a few clicks on the Internet, for many others, you can't. And many of those online transactions start with a salesperson chatting on the website, sending an email or text, or calling on the phone.

In most successful businesses, the best salespeople are valued and given great recognition and independence.

For example, I knew a salesman who worked for a specialty chemicals firm. At the pinnacle of his career, he worked an average of just three hours a day, three days a week. Thanks to his experience, he made a lot of sales and was rewarded handsomely. Other staff were jealous, but the company managers were fine with this arrangement and valued him greatly because he produced results. If you want to, you can become like him.

CORE INSIGHTS TO TAKE AWAY

- Salespeople are hugely important. All business revolves around sales.

- Whatever motivates you is good.

- You need to want to go into sales.

- Keep your motivation in mind always – especially when the going gets tough.

WHAT NOT TO DO

If you can't find a good reason, don't go into sales. Don't even waste time trying. You would be neither successful nor happy.

PROFESSIONAL TIP

Mentally picture what you want to achieve. Visualize it. Creating a specific picture in your mind is a great tool for success because it programs your brain to focus on attaining that desire.

Do you want a new car? A better house for your family? Send your kids to college? Maybe you just want to make enough money so that nobody can tell you what to do. Or like me, you want to be debt-free. Perhaps you want to be Number

One in your field, so imagine your boss presenting you with the company's Top Achiever of the Year award. Maybe it's not a thing but a feeling. Ideally, it's both.

Print out a picture symbolizing your goal and look at it in the mirror every morning or place it on your desk at work. Imagine how proud, relieved, satisfied, or happy you'll feel when you've achieved this.

ACTION STEPS

1. Identify your motivation (or motivations). Write it down.

2. Tell one or several people about it. Be careful not to tell negative people but only supportive, positive people. Each time you meet them, you'll remember what you told them – and they may even remind you and inquire about your progress.

CHAPTER 2

UNDERSTAND YOUR PRODUCT

It was crunch time. The buyer had a round of questions he needed answers to before he invested in the fund. And this buyer had a reputation for being demanding and thorough. Also, he had major influence in the market, so if he invested, others would follow.

He requested an impromptu conference call with some follow-up questions before his investment committee the next day. I was in an airport. Luckily my flight was delayed, but I still had to hang around the gate with lots of distracting background noise. This was the only time I've ever hoped that a flight would be delayed longer, so I could make the call.

I dialed in to the conference bridge with a colleague who was in a different location, then connected with the two members of the buying team. We had already sent them around 1,000 pages of follow-up material, which they had reviewed. They might have questions on that, or anything else they had forgotten to ask us.

I apologized for the background noise. "No problem," the buyers said and thanked us for being available on short notice. Then they plowed ahead with what seemed like the cross-examination from hell. We listened hard and answered thoroughly.

Then came a question about an hour into the call.

"We already answered that question," I said politely. "It's on page 56 of the material we sent over, about halfway down the page."

I didn't have the documents in front of me – but I was sure I had the page correct, because I had written and assembled the documentation myself.

There was a pause. They knew that I didn't have the document in front of me.

Then, "Wow, there it is," one of them said half laughing. "That's impressive. You know your stuff."

At that moment, I knew we would close, and we did because I *did* know my stuff. And my knowledge of what I was selling established my credibility.

Understanding your product or service and the role it plays in the market is the key that unlocks the door to success. Your product or service is part of an economic ecosystem. What role can your product play in this system? Find that role, and help the product fulfill it to your utmost ability.

I'm using the word *product* for whatever you're selling, whether that's a physical item or a service.

HOW I SOLD CABIN RENTALS IN AN UNPOPULAR SPOT

Muffin's cabin business was set away from Lake Winnipesaukee. We didn't have a lot that customers might want:

- We didn't have a lake-shore property.

- We weren't in the thick of a popular spot, but at the end of a strip of hotels.

- We didn't have a pool.

- We didn't have air conditioning.

- We didn't have color TV. In fact, we had 6 cabins when I started and only 3 portable black and white TVs, which we rented out separately.

- Our cabins were old. Built by my great-grandmother in the 1920s, they were seriously out of date by 1982.

This was the reality our family faced. We couldn't change any of these features immediately – and many couldn't be changed at all. We had to find a way to sell what we had.

We set out to identify advantages. In the days before the Internet and easy online research, we drove around, we looked, we asked questions. Sometimes, we pretended we were renters. When customers stayed, we asked them if they visited other places and encouraged them to tell us how we compared.

We found that our cabins had several advantages. In fact, many of our competitive advantages were simply the "drawbacks" viewed from a fresh perspective.

- We were set back from the main tourist area, so it was a quiet spot – ideal for visitors seeking peace and calm.

- We didn't have many facilities, which meant we had lower overhead compared to the competition – so we could charge the lowest price.

- Our cabins' age gave them a quaint, historical feel.

- We didn't have a lot of amenities to our cabins, but cleanliness was within our control – and thanks to my sister, our cabins were super clean.

- We were a family business, and this gave people a sense of connection.

That last point proved to be crucial because people subconsciously seek a connection, which leads, ultimately, to a relationship. This is a deep-rooted human need. I made the most of this.

When cars drove up our driveway, I walked out and greeted the customers while they were still in the car.

- I was cheerful. "Good afternoon! How are you today?" This allowed them to stay in the car while I told them what we had.

- In the meantime, I could assess what kind of customers they were. (More about that in Chapter 3.)

- I could also disarm their reservations and sell them the positives:

  "We run a quiet spot here." (Maybe they hadn't thought this was important until I mentioned it. It certainly meant they weren't disappointed when they realized they were away from the lively center.)

  "Yes, these cabins *are* old, my great-grandmother built them in 1927." (This gave them the feeling that they were staying in a piece of history.)

Today, this is called the "customer experience." But back then, I was simply happy that people were considering our cabins, and this enthusiasm spread to the customer.

Also, in 1982, before *transparent* was a buzzword, we were transparent. We insisted that everyone look at the cabin before renting so they knew what they were getting.

DIFFERENTIATING

In what way is your product different from your competitors'? To some prospective buyers, this difference presents a drawback; to others, it's an advantage.

Don't hide the difference, even if you think it's a weakness. Instead, find the kind of buyer who will value the difference, then emphasize it. Having a product that's different from all the others will increase the chances of your success.

Your confidence in the characteristic will help persuade the buyer.

BECOME A VALUE-ADDED RESOURCE IN THE SALES PROCESS

Later, when I sold private equity funds, product knowledge was even more important. I learned this principle from my mentor and partner, Arthur Gartland. Art is an intense man. A former Marine Corps A6 pilot, he brought that same level of intensity and thoroughness to his investment banking business.

In our business – the private fund placement agent business – there are typically two types of professionals: project managers and salespeople. Project managers conduct the due diligence on the investment manager and the fund and write the marketing material. They're product specialists. Then they pass the deal on to the salespeople, who make calls, meet with investors, and close them. Art didn't believe in keeping the two roles separate. When he picked a team, they had to do everything, which, by necessity, made all the salespeople experts in the deal, the ultimate product specialists.

So, before we sold anybody's product, we spent a lot of time on due diligence, getting to know the product and its background, meeting with the people at the fund manager's office, and understanding their investment philosophy and track record. We had several reasons for doing this:

- We wanted to understand their business and product from every angle and make sure that what they were telling us was accurate.

- In some cases, we identified sales and marketing points that the fund manager was unaware of or had never considered.

- When speaking with investors in the market, we could modulate our conversation to fit the situation. We had the knowledge to either have a superficial conversation about basic points or a meaningful substantive discussion covering every aspect the client wanted to discuss.

Many salespeople are good at that superficial type conversation which is usually enough for a first meeting, and some of them have made it through their careers without going beyond. But the more comprehensive your knowledge, the more added value you can bring to the sales process. And this is what you'll need to survive. (This book is about survival, not being lucky!)

You don't have to use all this knowledge. The purpose isn't to be a "smarty-pants." The purpose is to give the buyer the information they need to make a decision in your favor.

Knowing your product or service inside and out comes with a bonus: you'll automatically be more confident. When you've completely internalized this information, you become an expert, and this is often very attractive to buyers.

CORE INSIGHTS TO TAKE AWAY

- Extensive product/service knowledge makes you an expert and a value-added component in the sales process.

- Don't worry about what you don't have. Sell what you have.

- Consider your product's drawbacks – and then look at the other side of the coin. What are the advantages?

- Differentiate your product. Know what makes it unusual and capitalize on that.

- Know your product and all relevant material so well that you can answer almost any question about it in any situation.

- People want to connect. Find a way to connect and establish a relationship.

WHAT NOT TO DO

- Don't be a smarty-pants. Don't start spewing information out just to show how knowledgeable you are. The purpose of your knowledge is to establish credibility and give the buyer the information they need to make a decision in your favor.

- While differentiating, don't badmouth your competitors and their products. Don't say things like "I hear they're losing investors" or "Their products don't last long." Beating up or tearing down your competitors would make you come across as insecure and petty. This doesn't convey confidence.

PROFESSIONAL TIP

What's relevant to the sale is situational. Figure out what's important in that moment and adapt your strategy.

With our cabin-renting business, we used two different approaches because customers arrived with two different kinds of needs.

During the week, we sought the lowest price point at which we could fill our six (later eight) cabins. So, I hung out a price on our sign, say "$19 for 2" on a Sunday, to get as many people to drive up as possible. The more people drove up, the greater the chance of filling up. I put up the "Vacancy" sign early in the morning, even if we didn't have a single cabin cleaned yet, just to get people in. Sunday was our slowest day. As the week went on I would gradually increase the price each day until the weekend.

On the weekend, our approach was the opposite. We opened as late as possible at the price point we wanted. On Saturday afternoons, we might wait until 4pm before we announced our vacancies. Why? By that time, all the other local cabins and hotels were full. People who needed a place to stay didn't care whether we had a pool or color TV. All that mattered was that we had a vacancy. Now we could charge three or four times what our baseline Sunday price was.

In business terminology, we aimed to be a revenue maximizer during the week and a profit maximizer on the weekend. It worked.

That's when I learned an important principle: What's relevant to the sale is situational. You have to figure out what's important in that moment.

On Monday, if a traveler visited us at 4:15pm, maybe they wanted a pool and cable TV and maybe they wanted to walk to the beach. We weren't the spot for them.

On Saturday at 4:15pm, the same person had just spent an hour looking for a place, any place, with a vacancy in the area and just needed a place to stay. Suddenly, a clean, rustic cabin was the perfect fit, and customers were willing to pay the higher price.

ACTION STEPS

1. Make a list of attributes for what your selling. Include not just what your company gives you, think of some others. Ask some existing customers. This will be a "living list." As you hear more, you add to the list.

2. Now let's practice for the situational sale. Imagine sitting with a customer who's interested in your product but has already looked at your competitor's which he thinks is probably better. As he extols the virtues of the competing product, acknowledge the difference – and present it as a benefit.

Here are some examples:

Customer: "They have a pool and you don't."

You: "Yeah. If you stay here with us, you pay less per night. Just drive down to the beach if you want to swim and buy yourself a steak dinner with the money you save."

* * * *

Customer: "Their hotel has a more convenient location, close to the town center and main roads."

You: "That's true. But it's more peaceful and quiet here. You won't be bothered by traffic noise and loud music at night."

* * * *

Customer: "Their restaurant has a more extensive menu."

You: "You're right. That's because we only offer homemade food. My grandmother is in charge of the kitchen, and she cooks everything fresh every day."

CHAPTER 3

UNDERSTANDING YOUR BUYERS

Cindy (not her real name) worked as a senior investment professional at a prominent foundation. I had sent her information on the Asian Fund and had followed up several times. She left me a voicemail acknowledging receipt and saying that while it was interesting, it wasn't interesting enough to meet.

I was unconcerned. Although the fundraising had started slowly, it was already accelerating. This fund would reach its sales target without Cindy.

One day, the phone rang. It was Cindy. "Hi, Patrick. Are you still in the market with that Asian Fund?"

"Yes," I confirmed. "But we're almost done. We only have $10 million left."

"I'll take it!"

This was unusual. Cindy typically required a meeting and

some follow-up before making a decision. This time, there were no probing questions, no hesitation, no meetings. She simply bought.

What changed Cindy's attitude? I'll show you the answer later in this chapter, so read on.

Let's explore the world of the buyers. At the center of all sales work are buyers – the clients, customers, investors, service users, subscribers, whatever your organization calls them. Without buyers, there can be no sales. So, treat them with consideration and dignity.

Buyers are people. Do you generally like people? I hope you do, because that's what selling is about. If you don't, perhaps you should consider a different career. Sure, there are some salespeople of the predator type who disdain their fellow human beings and still make a career. I don't know how they do it because I choose to not hang out with their sort. There are also some forms of sales where you need to interact only a little or only over a distance such as online. But most sales ultimately require some form of human interaction, and that's the focus of this book.

You don't need to like buyers the way you like friends. You don't need to agree with their ethics, politics, or religion. But you need to like them as fellow human beings and give them your interest and respect. It's a professional relationship.

BUYER, CUSTOMER, OR CLIENT?

The terminology varies from field to field: shops have customers, restaurants have patrons, consultants have clients. Others have service users, patients, subscribers, guests, or investors.

Sometimes, you may even serve two different groups. For example, in our placement agent business, we're selling to "investors" on behalf of fund managers whom we call "clients." Don't let the words confuse you.

In this book, I'll keep things simple. I'll use the term *buyers* for anyone who buys, has bought, or may buy something from you.

RETAIL BUYERS

Retail buyers self-select. They choose to come to your business, so you know they have some level of interest in what you have to offer. You figure out whether there's a fit, and how much they want your product.

Renting cabins taught me how to deal with retail buyers. When they came up the driveway, I knew that they were almost certainly looking to rent a cabin.

Showing them an available cabin allowed me to establish rapport and to find out more about what they wanted. Simple questions like "How's your vacation going?" and "What have you been doing?" weren't merely a courtesy, but showed the customers that I cared, and, more importantly, gave me clues about their needs.

I also learned to assess what mattered to different types of people.

If a Harley rider arrived with his girlfriend, they probably just wanted a place with a double bed and a shower. So, I showed those features, and didn't bother the couple with the history of the place or information about local attractions.

On the other hand, if a family with a young child drove up, I asked, "Have you tried the waterslide down the street? I think we have some coupons for that."

Perhaps a couple mentioned that they were antiquing for the week. I could hook them by saying, "My great-grandmother built this cabin in the 1920s."

A useful question was, "Have you been looking for a place to stay for a while?" If the customers replied that they had, this revealed that they didn't know yet what they actually wanted, so I probed further: "Really? What have you seen so far?" This allowed me to figure out what was important to them: price, ambiance, location?

When they viewed, I pointed out the relevant good points, emphasizing the aspects they had found lacking in other venues. "Pretty simple, clean. Nice and quiet here at night." If they liked the cabin, I got them signed in.

BUSINESS-TO-BUSINESS

Selling private equity funds turned out to be a whole different matter. The people we were selling to could rarely decide on the spot. (Which is why Cindy's behavior was so unusual. Answer still to come, keep reading!) More often, the process involved a whole team, some of whom I might never even meet, and I had to win over all of them.

I learned two important factors about buyers in a business-to-business sale:

- The buyer doesn't want to look stupid.

- The buyer doesn't want to lose his job as a result of making the purchase.

The biggest risk on business-to-business sales is the buyer's career risk.

Understand this. Put yourselves in the buyer's shoes – nervous about how this purchase will affect his career – and listen to your pitch. Would you buy this from yourself?

Now let's consider the pitch. Your pitch. There are really two components to it: the rational and the emotional. You need to be prepared to address both to get to a point of trust and a position in which you can close.

The "rational" is made up of all the facts and figures and the compelling arguments you make on the phone, in person, and in your promotional material. We covered this in the previous chapter when we looked at your product.

The "emotional" addresses or satisfies an emotion they feel surrounding the sale.

RECOGNIZING BUYERS' ATTITUDES

Here are some emotion-laden attitudes you may encounter when selling investments:

- Greedy. They want to make a ton of money and are worried less about the risk of losing all their investment.

- Frightened. They're afraid of losing any money.

- Wanting to be popular. They want to be in all investments that the "players" in their space are in, irrespective of risk or return.

- Cutting edge. They don't mind taking calculated risks on new ideas and being the first or early into an exciting new investment space. To them, it's a thrilling adventure.

- Risk-averse. They only want proven products with long track records on established, stable strategies.

You may encounter each of these emotional attitudes separately, or a buyer may display two or more of them. Depending on your business, you may also encounter variations.

Sometimes, I'm explicit about addressing the emotion. If a potential buyer shows signs of being frightened and risk-averse, I may say something like this: "I'm also afraid of where we are in the market right now, and that's why I'm representing this fund manager. They're conservative and prudent investors."

As well as their emotional attitude, I assess their personality types. Of the many personality-typing systems, I find the DISC approach the most practical. DISC divides people into four basic categories: Dominance, Influence, Steadiness, and Conscientious.

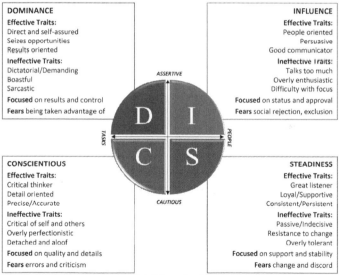

Courtesy of Eckfeldt & Associates/Based on the DISC theory of psychologist William Moulton Marston

A Dominance person may be completely comfortable making a decision alone. You can be direct: "Is this something you're interested in?"

An Influence person may be more concerned with the opinions of colleagues or industry peers. "I have a list of industry leaders who use our service, would you like to see it?"

A Steadiness person will deliberate before any decision. "Why don't you take some time to digest all this information? How about I call you back three weeks from today at 2pm?"

And a Conscientious person will put much more emphasis on the "rational" part of the sales decision. "We have a more detailed data sheet that I'll send you. Then let's do a follow-up call next Thursday morning to go through it, okay?"

Don't be dogmatic with this information. People can have multiple attributes, but one or two tend to dominate. For example, I tend towards Conscientious first and Dominance second.

Obviously, you'll adapt your questions to your specific business. The point is that you can usually get a sense of who these people are early in a conversation by listening carefully to the questions they ask and the answers they give, and then adjust your pitch accordingly.

Often, a team is involved in making the purchase decision, so you may have multiple personalities to deal with. One friend in corporate sales describes this as "solving a complex puzzle." Try to identify a team member who will take responsibility and be an advocate. I've heard this person referred to as a "champion," but I don't like that label because it implies that the person is going to push the sale through for you. I prefer the term *advocate* because it links in with the insight that buyers don't want to take huge career risks.

An advocate won't do your job for you, but she'll help you do your job more effectively. For example, she may give you some coaching or guidance. She may also tell you that someone on the team has a misconception that needs to be addressed. Perhaps she tips you off that while a certain set of priorities is articulated in a group setting, a different set of priorities is being focused on behind the scenes. She can let you know what sort of impact the purchase will have on her organization: this is good for Bill and his team but makes life hard in Nancy's department.

The advocate isn't necessarily one of the senior people on the team. Sometimes, it's a junior person – so remember to be respectful to everyone on the buying team and keep the lines of communication open at all levels.

Which brings us back to Cindy. Who was she?

You might think Cindy was a Conscientious person based on past behavior. I certainly did up until her call. But Cindy was an Influence person. As the Asian Fund became more popular and sales accelerated, she heard about it from her peers. What was her biggest fear? Exclusion from a popular fund.

CORE INSIGHTS TO TAKE AWAY

- Buyers are people. Treat them with dignity.

- Try to establish a rapport to find out what's important to the buyer.

- Put yourself in the position of the buyer.

- Career risk governs most business-to-business purchasing decisions.

- Build trust by addressing the rational and emotional aspects of the sale.

- Buyers have different personality types. Adjust your pitch and expectations accordingly.

WHAT NOT TO DO

- Don't ignore what retail buyers are telling you, even if they're waffling about seemingly irrelevant subjects. They're really telling you how you can sell to them.

- Don't be aggressive. Aggression means that you don't care about the person on the other side of the table, only about making a sale at any price. While aggression may resonate with the Dominance character, it tends to be a turn-off for almost everyone else.

Assertiveness, on the other hand, is good. Assertive means

you do understand the buyers' position and you're strongly communicating why you think this sale is in their best interest. The difference between "assertiveness" and "aggression" may seem small, but to the person on the receiving end, it feels big.

PROFESSIONAL TIP

If a prospect turns out not to be a buyer because what you offer doesn't match her needs, treat her with courtesy anyway. Give her a good experience she'll remember. She may become a buyer in the future, or she may recommend your product to others.

When people viewed one of our cabins and didn't like it, I aimed to be super-helpful. "Okay, what are you looking for? Ah, you want a pool? Drive this way for a mile. There are three places in a row with a pool."

You know what? They sometimes came back. "We went and saw some other places, but we liked it here better."

I created a positive experience, even though they said "No." That left the door open for them to return.

Another reason to create a positive experience: word-of-mouth recommendations are a salesperson's dream, and you can get them by being super helpful to buyers irrespective of their immediate decision.

ACTION STEPS

This assignment requires you to use your imagination.

First, decide what product or service you want to pitch for this exercise. If possible, make it one you're currently selling or planning to sell.

Pick one of the DISC personality types (Dominance, Influence, Conscientious, or Steadiness) – perhaps that reflects your own nature best. Imagine you're a buyer with that type and interested in the product. What would you like to hear in a sales pitch? What would make you feel good, rouse your interest, whet your desire? Write it down.

Now repeat the assignment for the other three personality types. You may want to take a short break between each to clear your brain, because switching between personalities in quick succession isn't easy.

Finally, create a generic pitch for a buyer whose personality type isn't known. This will probably be less effective than the specific ones, but it should still be good. Above all, it must not contain a turn-off for any of the types.

Now you have five pitches.

When pitching to a business owner, there's a pretty good chance you can start with your D pitch. A person in the marketing department is most likely an I. For a bureaucrat, try the S pitch, and for an engineer, a C. Then listen to clues, and switch if necessary.

If you have no idea, you can always apply the generic version.

CHAPTER 4

PRACTICE MAKES NATURAL

Ben (not his real name) was a busy man, a thorough person leading a very understaffed investment department. We had reached the final part of the negotiation on a fund in which his firm would be the largest investor. Ben's company wrote big checks. We wanted Ben and we wanted Ben's investment.

He had postponed on me twice already. I didn't want to keep calling and seem desperate. So, I waited and waited… and staying patient can be the toughest part of the sales job.

After eight days, Ben finally rang and apologized for taking so long to call me back; he had been swamped.

It was after business hours on a hot and humid summer day. I was in the park, sweaty and uncomfortable. In the background, kids were screaming as they played. This wasn't the ideal situation for a crucial telephone conversation.

This wasn't an ideal situation for me, but you know what? I was okay because I was ready. I had already practiced this conversation dozens of times, just without Ben being there!

So, I just started. We had a lot of back and forth but eventually found common ground. When I hung up the phone, I sat on a park bench, and typed up the terms we had discussed in an email to Ben just so we were both clear on what we had agreed. He confirmed almost immediately.

Selling needs to become a natural state in which you know what to do without consciously thinking about the specific details every moment.

Obviously, experience helps. But when you're just starting out, how do you get to that state?

In this chapter, I'm sharing some approaches that have helped me. Try them – you'll probably find they work for you, too.

GET YOUR PRACTICE BEFORE YOU MEET YOUR BUYER

When you're face to face with a buyer isn't the time to think about what you should do. It has to come naturally.

You need to give your full attention to the customer, not to try to remember instructions. "Okay, what did Patrick say in his book – something about the rational sale and emotional sale... And the sales manager said to look them in the eye and shake their hand firmly but not too hard...wait, was I too hard? Oh dear, I forgot to say hello and use his name. I've got to work that in, when should I do that? We're sitting down now, is it too late?"

Practice beforehand to avoid this sort of panicked scrambling so that when you're in a selling situation, your reactions are natural and genuine. You want to be aware of what you're doing, but not self-conscious.

Here are the two most effective methods:

- Role-play.

- Record yourself.

ROLE-PLAYING

For role-playing, ask a coworker or friend to play the role of buyer, while you act the part of the salesperson.

If your fellow actor is also in sales, that's ideal, since he can mimic typical customer behavior and give you constructive feedback, and you can return the favor by playing buyer for his sales pitch.

However, your foil doesn't need to be a sales expert. Anyone who is willing to give a few minutes of their time to help you out is great. And if you don't find a partner, you can still practice by imagining the client sitting in that empty chair.

When you role-play, map out different scenarios for calls and meetings:

The average buyer in an average situation: Although no sales meeting ever plays out to a "norm" and how you expect it, imagine one that goes smoothly. The customer is interested and cooperative, you're in good form, and everything goes well. I recommend starting with this before you progress to role-playing specific scenarios.

The skeptical buyer: She challenges every point you make. Focus on practicing how you'll counter the challenge without sounding defensive.

The jerk: Your role-play partner behaves in an unpleasant, unprofessional way. Practice staying professional and not rising to the provocations.

Getting back on track: Imagine you've just spent twenty minutes talking about the Super Bowl last night (or dog breeding, global warming, the buyer's children). Now you need to get the buyer focused on your product again, but he wants to keep discussing the Super Bowl. How do you steer him back to the purpose of the conversation?

As you progress, you can add other scenarios from your experience. Your role-play partner can also contribute situations she's experienced.

Include a role-play where you are a buyer interested in your own product. Thinking like your own buyers can be a real eye-opener.

The purpose of the role-play is to put you under pressure. Don't waste the opportunity by fooling around. Take the role-play as seriously as a genuine sales conversation.

Once you've experienced the pressure in a simulated situation, you'll have the emotional "muscle memory" to react appropriately in a real environment.

RECORD YOURSELF

Record yourself. Your phone and your laptop probably have audio-recording functions. Start by simply saying a few sentences about a subject you're comfortable talking about. Then progress to describing your product's features and benefits and, finally, to speaking your actual sales pitch and answering customer questions.

Play back the audio. How do you sound? Perhaps you need to slow down as you talk, speak more clearly, or lower the tone of your voice.

You may cringe when you hear yourself. That's normal. Many people dislike their voice. The purpose of this exercise isn't to give you the sonorous tones of a professional narrator, but to modify your voice a little.

I'm self-conscious about my nasal voice, and when I get excited, I start to speak too quickly. I can't change my voice – it's part of who I am. But I make a conscious effort to slow down when things get intense.

Record what you say in voicemail messages especially. Early in my career, people called me back, saying, "I got your voicemail, but you were talking really fast and I didn't really hear what you were saying."

You can change your messages to see what works. Experiment with leaving little information or a lot. Play with the cadence of your message. Which version sounds best? That's the one to use. Once you've mastered the audio part, film yourself either explaining the product to the camera or role-playing the whole sales talk with a partner. The logistics may need some thought – where do you place your smartphone to film the whole interaction? – but it's worth doing, because you'll gain valuable insights that will improve your approach.

If you have great self-confidence and think you're already doing really well, ask yourself if there's something you can do even better.

If you're insecure and self-critical, don't use the recordings to beat yourself up. Instead, look for what works and resolve to build that into your real sales interactions. Only then, consider what you can do differently.

DON'T AIM FOR PERFECTION

Don't try to get everything "perfect." That's not necessary. Just aim to act naturally and confidently. You don't need to achieve an Oscar-worthy performance, merely to increase your chances of success.

I've had sales conversations when I did everything "perfectly" – pitch, presentation, body language, voice, persuasive arguments – and not closed.

I've also had bumbling interactions when I was self-conscious, stuttered, fumbled, and thought all was lost – yet still managed to close the sale.

CORE INSIGHTS TO TAKE AWAY

- Practice various situations, so you know how to respond when they arise.

- Aim to come across as confident and natural, not perfect and rehearsed.

- Your delivery doesn't have to be flawless. But it needs to be good.

WHAT NOT TO DO

- Don't worry if you make little "mistakes" like forgetting what you meant to say, stammering, not finding the document you meant to show. You're human, and your customers will appreciate talking with a real person and not a perfect machine.

- Don't practice every sentence until it sounds unnatural and rehearsed.

- Don't waste role-play opportunities to joke around. You're a professional: act like one.

PROFESSIONAL TIP

As you grow more experienced, move your role-playing practice to the next level. Ask a fellow salesperson to represent the customer in a specific important sales conversation you have coming up. You can even ask them to mimic "difficult" (impatient, unpleasant, hostile) buyers. If you familiarize yourself with the tricky situations, they won't throw you off balance when they happen.

Make a video of yourself making a presentation to understand what your face and body are doing when talking.

If you're like me, you'll be self-conscious and learn a lot about yourself.

ACTION STEPS

1. Record a one-minute story of your life, either audio or video. One minute only! Not your whole life story. Listen to this. Is your voice confident, pleasant, easy to understand? If not, modify it and record it again.

2. Record a voice-mail message in which you ask for a meeting. Listen to it and refine the content and tone until you're satisfied.

3. Find a role-playing partner (ideally another salesperson), schedule a session, and agree on the scenario(s) you want to practice.

CHAPTER 5

GETTING STARTED

You know your product. You have an idea about how buyers will receive it. Now it's time to sell.

Does the thought scare you?

You're not alone. Feeling intimidated is normal – It's like the thrill before a bungee jump – but you have to take that leap.

Some new salespeople enjoy the thrill of meeting their first buyer, while others would rather put it off. Try to be the former. Admit your fear but do it anyway – and try to enjoy the scary experience. Get comfortable with being a little uncomfortable.

HOW I GOT STARTED IN EARNEST

After selling cabin rentals for the family business for five years, I left my family business to enroll at the University of Chicago. While I was still studying at the University of Chicago, an alumnus, Jim Amen, recruited me to work for Philo Smith & Co. where he was a Managing Director.

Philo Smith interviewed and hired me personally. He was an expert on insurance companies, had written the first book in the U.S. on insurance company analysis in the 1960s and ran a hedge fund that invested solely in insurance company stocks. I wasn't aware of my luck at the time, but, in hindsight, I couldn't have asked for a better experience.

First, the company was small with six people, which suited my small-business personality. Second, although they intended to groom me for a sales position, they also trained me as an analyst, and my trainer was their best analyst, Sandra Pagel. In my three years at Philo Smith & Co., I was writing analytical reports on insurance companies as well as selling. This gave me enormous product knowledge.

Third, they were willing to do whatever it took to raise more money for their hedge fund. Without hesitation, Philo himself opened his Rolodex of contacts to me.

I started out with six leads from Philo and a phone. I practiced my pitch with him. Then I sent out information on our hedge fund and started calling senior insurance company and investment executives.

One person on that first list was Jack Byrne, a legend in the insurance and investment business. I left him a message and he promptly returned my call. I can only imagine how awkward my newbie pitch sounded to Mr. Byrne! But you know what? He listened patiently and asked a couple questions. Ultimately, he passed: "We like to roll our own here, Patrick, but thank you."

It was a "No" – but what a beautiful one! I had engaged an investment professional at the highest level without completely embarrassing myself. In fact, I felt like I had gotten close to a "Yes." The adrenaline was rushing. This was the place for me!

That summer, I was hooked. While most of my peers at university did meaningless make-work intern jobs at big firms, I got to talk with highly experienced investment professionals. I knew that if I stuck with it, I would achieve success. I didn't see it so clearly at the time, but I was committing to a process.

Only seven months before, I had dreaded getting stuck in a management consultancy career that didn't suit me. Now, when I went back for the second year of my MBA, I had an agreement with Philo Smith & Co. that I would work for them part time out of my apartment and had a full-time job with them when I graduated. What a dramatic shift in my expectations!

Philo gave me a loose-leaf binder to keep notes in. I used it prolifically. When I left a message with someone, I jotted down the date. After every conversation I had, I made notes of what we had talked about, including why they said "No" or passed.

That's how I got started. Now it's your turn. Are you itching to start or still trying to hide?

Getting started means acting.

It means calling someone up, sending an email, knocking on a door, sending a letter, going to a conference, arranging a demonstration for your product, and initiating contact in whatever way you can.

Getting started also means:

- Not being afraid to make mistakes.

- Not being afraid of rejection.

- A commitment to learning from rejection.

I didn't fully realize how much I had learned until I moved to New York City and began working at Benedetto, Gartland & Co., which, for me, was the "big time." I was selling leveraged buyout funds to institutional investors like insurance companies (which I knew) but also banks, pension funds, and endowments, which were new to me.

At first, I was annoyed because in this firm, I didn't get an office like I had at Philo Smith & Co. I was out in the bullpen where I had to make calls out in the open. It felt like a demotion. Sometimes, it was so noisy, I would sit under my desk, talking on the phone to investors.

But even that frustrating situation had its benefits. People observed that I was fearless about calling up investors. The President's and the Chairman's offices were on either side of the bullpen – and they heard me pitching. Within a year, I had my own office again. I achieved this so fast simply because I learned about the products the firm offered and wasn't afraid to pick up the phone.

Another great thing about Benedetto, Gartland & Co was their customized computer CRM system. I moved from my notebooks to a computerized system in which all the salespeople could share what they had learned on a call or at a meeting. It took my tracking and education to a new level. When everyone shared information like this, we were all more powerful.

What's your objective when you make an introductory call or send an introductory email?

To make a sale?

Not so fast. Typically, that's unrealistic.

For me, it's not a sale – that comes later. During that initial phone conversation, my aim is simple engagement. They may not have looked at the material I sent them. If they haven't, then I give them a verbal summary. If they don't have time for that, I book a follow-up call. If they've read it, I find a time to meet. (More about that in Chapter 6)

If you don't have to achieve a sale on every call but merely to book a meeting, making that call is suddenly far less daunting, isn't it?

CORE INSIGHTS TO TAKE AWAY

- Sooner or later, you have to act and contact the buyer.

- It's normal to feel afraid or self-conscious. Don't let the fear stop you. Instead, try to enjoy the thrill.

- Have a reason and an objective for the call (e.g., following up on information sent, arrange a meeting if there's genuine interest).

- Commit to a process.

WHAT NOT TO DO

Don't continuously hide behind email. Speak to a real person, either on the phone or face to face.

PROFESSIONAL TIP

I tend to group calls into blocks of ten at a time. I don't think about much in between, don't dwell on either the negative or positive. Just do it, take notes, and do the next. Deconstructing/analyzing every call on the spot will slow your momentum and can create excuses not to keep going. Keep going!

ACTION STEPS

1. Make a list of the people you're going to contact.

2. Now contact them! All of them. Remember, you don't have to clinch a sale. You only need to achieve a smaller objective such as setting up an appointment.

3. Finished? Now make another list and do the same.

CHAPTER 6

PRACTICAL SALES TIPS

Here are some tactics and strategies that have worked for me and others. As you read this section, think about how you could apply them to your own sales.

ARRIVE EARLY

In our cabin business, I always tried to open early – unless it was a busy weekend when I purposely opened late to raise the prices.

As I came up through the ranks in Wall Street, I always tried to be in the office early. This quiet time allowed me to prepare for the day and get my head in the game before the phone started ringing.

If you need to reach executives, try calling at 8:30am or 5:30pm. Important executives often get into the office early and work late, and they appreciate people who operate in the same way. Once the office has emptied, there are also fewer matters competing for their attention.

When I plan trips, I aim to get to my destination well ahead of schedule, so if a delay occurs on the journey, it's not a disaster. I don't want to get stuck in a traffic jam or spend time in an airport waiting for a canceled flight to be rescheduled. I don't mind arriving early and having to kill time – but I don't want to arrive last minute, flustered and sweaty, or even worse, late.

I also reduce potential obstacles on the way to my destination. Where possible, I take direct flights, so I won't risk missing a connection.

BE OVERPREPARED.... EVEN MILDLY PARANOID

If I expect to meet twenty people over three days, I bring twenty-five presentation packs with me, just in case more people show up.

For important meetings at a buyer's office, I sometimes bring a copy of every document we have ever sent them.

BRING SAMPLES OR MODELS

Samples the buyer can touch, smell, and taste are more convincing than leaflets and brochures, so if possible, offer a sample.

If its portable equipment, a demonstration is often best. For large items such as buildings and machinery, three-dimensional models are useful. Buyers like to be able to view the miniature from different perspectives. Engineers tend to feel good if they have something they can get their hands on and understand.

MATCHING BODY LANGUAGE

Aim to match the other person's body language. If they lean forward, lean forward too. Subconsciously, they'll perceive that you're on the same wavelength. But don't overdo this. Mimicking their every movement will feel like mockery, and they'll resent you for it.

SMILE

Your smile puts people at ease and makes them like you.

Make it a genuine smile, not a fake one. Did you know that most people can sense if a smile is fake or genuine? A real smile does more than turn up the corners of the mouth. It lights up your whole face.

How do you achieve that?

1. Think a genuine positive thought about the person you're meeting. Think, *I'm pleased to meet her* or, *What a great opportunity for me!*

2. Smile with your eyes. Imagine switching on a smile behind your eyes, like turning on a light. If you imagine it, it will happen. When you smile with your eyes, the mouth follows. Try it: the effects are phenomenal.

DO FAVORS AND ASK FOR FAVORS

Be helpful. Watch out for opportunities to assist a buyer.

Often, you can help by simply providing information. Many buyers operate in their own vacuum. You, on the other hand, are out in the market, talking to everyone. This gives you a big advantage. You may have access to precisely the data a buyer needs to persuade her superiors.

Perhaps the buyer has a problem in another part of his business, and you can provide a useful introduction. Maybe it has nothing to do with business. One buyer found out I had played rugby. Since his son had recently become interested in the sport, he needed some guidance.

Conversely, don't be afraid to ask for favors. Most people enjoy being helpful, and if they can do you a small favor, it will make them feel good. Asking for a purchase order doesn't count as a favor asked! Look for something else – and it has to be something you're genuinely interested in and won't be any trouble at all for the other person.

Here are some examples.

"Oh, is that a such-and-such gadget? I've been thinking of buying one of these. Are you happy with it? May I take a look?"

"You speak Mandarin Chinese? I wonder if you could help me. I need to write this sentence in Mandarin."

"I've been admiring the marigolds in your garden. I'm a passionate gardener myself and have never seen this variety. Do you mind if I take a few seeds?"

Favors asked make the person relate you and establish common ground.

DON'T BE AFRAID OF THE SILENCE

Many salespeople are often petrified when silence descends in a meeting. They start babbling desperately to fill the void.

But the silence often simply means that the buyer is processing what you've just said and needs a moment to think. Give him or her that time.

If you have to break the silence, ask a question, ideally one that doesn't interrupt the thought process. "Do you have any questions at this stage?" or "Was that clear?"

If you really need to press on, ask, "Shall we keep going?"

MEETING OVER A MEAL

Scheduling a sales meeting over a breakfast, lunch, or dinner can be a good move.

Personally, I'm not a huge fan of business meals. Sometimes, people don't concentrate on what is said, it can be difficult to hear what everyone is saying over the restaurant noises, and there isn't room on the table for presentation materials.

However, many salespeople swear by them. Eating is an enjoyable activity for most, so your potential buyers are probably in a relaxed, positive mood. The dialogue flows more freely. In addition, meetings over a meal are a way to sit down with people whose schedules are otherwise too crammed to fit you in.

CONVERSATION TOPICS

In building a relationship, you build a rapport with the buyer. But they don't just want to hear about what you have to sell. In fact, most people like to talk about themselves, so get to know them! Here are some subjects people like to talk about (even if it's just to complain):

- the weather

- their kids

- their pets

- their sports teams (unless the teams are embarrassingly bad)

- their vacations (recent or planned)

- their hobbies

Topics to avoid:

- politics

- religion

- an embarrassing mistake their company has just made (unless you're there to sell them a solution)

While chatting, establish common ground – but take care not to dominate the conversation. Instead, immediately ask an open-ended question to encourage the buyer to talk.

Examples:

"Oh, you have the new such-and-such smartphone. I have the previous model and am thinking of upgrading. What's your experience?"

"My kittens are two months old, just weaned. How old are yours?"

"You've just come back from Acapulco? My wife wants to go there for next year's vacation. What's it like?"

MAKE NOTES ON THE BUYER

For each buyer you meet and expect to meet again, jot down notes – not just about their buying preferences, but any private matters that come up. "Keen gardener, likes organic food. Has two boys, both into baseball. Collects fridge magnets. Plans to adopt a dog from an animal rescue shelter."

Before the next meeting, quickly flick through your notes to refresh your memory. The buyer will be pleased if you ask how her boys are doing and if she has found the right dog at the shelter. This creates a personal rapport.

HOW TO CONDUCT A SALES MEETING

In twenty-five years of investor meetings, I've learned useful techniques by trial and error. Here's a "blueprint" you can use and adapt, so you don't have to make the same mistakes yourself.

- Get to the meeting ten minutes early. Not an hour

early – that would seem desperate and waste your time – and not late – that would leave you flustered and give the impression that you're disrespectful or disorganized.

- Look people in the eye when you shake hands and repeat their name and yours. "Hi, Janet, I'm Patrick Campbell."

- Use a firm handshake. Limp handshakes come across as weak or insincere, but you shouldn't engage the customer in a power game or strength contest either.

- Our pitch meetings typically last between 45 minutes and an hour, but it's good to ask at the beginning, "How much time do we have?" Maybe the investor's schedule has gotten pushed back and you only have thirty minutes now. This is good to know, so you can adjust.

- Sometimes, people have read your material but, at other times, they haven't. They may have intended to but couldn't found the time. Some will even pretend to have read it, even though they haven't. I always ask, "Is there anything in particular you want us to cover today?" They may be specific about what they want, or they want you to lead them.

- Before the meeting, internalize the necessary information about the product. (See Chapter 2.) So, when you speak, it's conversational. If you give a presentation, refer to the material on the page, but avoid reading from the page. I always know what's there (many times I'm the one who wrote or cowrote it), so I can talk to the investor, not read the presentation to the investor with my head down.

- If other members of your company participate in the meeting, help them prepare. Provide them with information about the buyer, point out potential obstacles, warn them of any pitfalls. The last thing you want is a sales meeting where your most senior executive inadvertently steps on a landmine.

- It's natural for meetings to go off on tangents now and then. But time is precious, so don't let it go to waste. Don't be afraid to steer the meeting back to the topics that need to be discussed in the allotted time. Be upfront about it: "I just want to make sure we discuss these two topics before we run out of time, because we think they're important for you to understand."

- Bring the meeting to life. My father's company makes testing equipment, so every pitch is a practical demonstration of how a piece of equipment is used. If it's something you're going to customize, bring a sample. If you can't bring in what you do, use a case study, a real-life example with pictures. Now your pitch isn't just words; it's real.

- Make notes during the meeting. Date, name of firm,

who is attending. You don't have to transcribe everything that's said, but write down important points, buy signals, and concerns. Note how the buyer reacts to a topic (e.g., "doesn't care about feature X but loves Y").

- If someone else is doing the talking – perhaps your client or a colleague – look interested! Even if you've heard that sales pitch a hundred times, don't show boredom. No doodling, no daydreaming, no checking the text messages on your smartphone. Be attentive; otherwise, the buyers may think the pitch isn't worth listening to.

- When you're not talking, you're listening and observing. You're watching for body language and reactions. Do they look bored or confused? Are they still with you? It's okay to ask, "Was our last point clear?" and go back if necessary.

- If they're giving you feedback, let them talk. Then ask, "Is there anything else?"

- At the end of the meeting, recap what the follow-up steps are. If those haven't been specified, ask, "What are the next steps?" The more specific the steps, the more on track you are. Send a follow-up email articulating these next steps and any other action items.

Use this structure as a guide but be prepared to deviate from it if the situation calls for a different approach.

CLOSING

In our fund placement business, we compare closing a sale to a hurdles race. A line of hurdles are up ahead: getting a meeting, following up, having a second meeting, answering due diligence questions, legal review, operational due diligence, investment committee. We always focus on the hurdle in front of us. Taking one hurdle after the other, we finish the race.

The race is finished when we get a commitment from an investor. Sometimes, I'm patient… but when the situation calls for it, I'm a little pushy.

To close, you apply all your product and buyer knowledge as well as your experience to fulfill any special requests and remove any remaining objections one by one until you're left with a "Yes."

The "Yes" has to be from a person or team that's empowered to say "Yes."

What if a customer can't decide – or doesn't want to?

Some sales processes go on and on – and when they finally end, it's with a decision to delay the decision until another time. Perpetually delayed decisions are the bane of a salesperson's existence.

The best motivator for closing is a deadline – either yours or theirs. A deadline forces a decision one way or another. If you're dealing with a decision-delaying buyer, think in advance about a deadline you can bring up:

"The special offer ends on Monday."

"Your company needs this for the event, and it takes five days to manufacture, so today is the last day to place the order."

"I need to catch the train at 5:30."

ASKING FOR THE ORDER

There comes a time when you'll have to ask for the order, especially if the decision process has dragged on and nothing would be gained by going over the same ground yet again.

You may have a deadline and are running out of time. Perhaps your sales manager is pressing you for results. In my experience, it's best not to wait until the sales manager's patience runs out.

In such a situation I tell myself two things:

- "Sooner or later, you have to ask."

- "Don't be afraid of the 'No.'"

WHAT TO DO WHEN A CUSTOMER SAYS "NO"

Most of the time the "No" is a "No."

But if you've had a substantive interaction with the customer, it's reasonable for you to ask, "Why?"

Perhaps the customer likes the competitor's product better. In this case, knowing the reasons will give you useful insights.

Maybe the customer can't afford the product right now because their budget is almost spent. In this case, you may still be able to offer a cheaper alternative, arrange financing, or visit them again in the next budget period.

Maybe there was a misunderstanding about some feature or aspect of what you've offered. In my experience, if you get the "No" because of a misunderstanding, you have 24 hours to turn it around. The buyer is in decision-making mode and they have made an uninformed decision, so you have to clear this up immediately before they tell someone else "Yes." Here's how I do it: I drop everything and bring in as many resources as quickly as possible to clarify whatever the misunderstanding was. Do whatever it takes: get on the phone, get on a plane, bring in anyone necessary – the top engineer, the president of your company, the portfolio manager, the head designer, your grandmother… just get your foot in the door before it closes, because once the "No" settles in, it becomes accepted.

On several occasions, buyers left "No" voicemails for me – and the reasons they gave were so feeble, they made no sense at all. When I called them back the next morning, I found they had gone on vacation for two weeks. These people had experience and knew how to avoid justifying their decision. Such situations are frustrating. But frankly, these people wouldn't have bought anyway, so it's just as well I didn't waste more time on them.

SAYING NO TO A BUYER

Once in a while, you have to say "No" to the buyer.

At our cabin business, sometimes a bunch of young people were looking for a place to party for the night, I would just tell them, "This is probably not the place for you." It saved both of us the hassle of a confrontation later in the evening.

In the private funds business, there are suitability rules. Often, investors will refer their wealthy friends. On more than one occasion, after speaking with a few of these people, it was clear to me that they didn't understand the risk or nature of what the private fund was doing. Usually, I asked them enough questions to lead them to the conclusion that this investment wasn't for them. And if they didn't come to the conclusion, I just came out and said that the investment was unsuitable for them and they couldn't invest.

It's okay to say "No" to a customer for the right reasons.

GIFT GIVING

I work in a regulated business that has very specific rules about gift giving. That's because, in some historical cases, the "gift" to the buyer was so generous that it was considered a bribe. So, now there are rules. Most firms now have rules on what and how much they will give as a gift.

You may know from previous meetings that this buyer is partial to chocolate or loves fresh fruit. Does she collect stamps or foreign coins? You may have some lying around at home from your last vacation, items of little monetary value that she would appreciate.

A gift can be a simple gesture. For example, if you're on your way to a meeting and stop by Starbucks, you call the buyer you're meeting with to ask her if she wants a cup of coffee as well.

Some firms have complex gifting programs in which they send out a company gift with their corporate logo printed on it. Such gifts can create goodwill for the company but may not stimulate personal warmth between the buyer and you.

For me, a gift is from the heart, and if I give a gift, I like it to be personal. In my opinion, John Ruhlin has written the best book on professional gifting, and you'll find it in the Recommended Reading section at the end of the book.

WHAT NOT TO DO

- Don't skimp on preparations. Arrive overprepared rather than underprepared.

- Don't schedule your arrival at the last minute. Allow for traffic jams, delayed flights, losing your way, and other unexpected problems.

- Don't allow buyers to delay a decision perpetually.

PROFESSIONAL TIP

When a buyer says "No," view this as an opportunity for a

future sale. People tend to remember the experience rather than the product you're selling at that moment. Stay professional.

The same person may buy from you in the future when their budget or their requirements have changed. They may even buy from you immediately if you offer a different product more suited to their current needs.

Even if they never buy anything from you, they may suggest your product to someone else.

And even if their firm never buys anything from your firm, you may meet this person years later when you both represent different companies, and, this time, they'll buy.

ACTION STEPS

1. Make a list of preparations for your next sales meeting. What will you need? What might you need? What could possibly come in useful? Include items for your personal use as well as for the presentation. What do you need to do beforehand?

2. Create a master checklist to consult whenever you prepare for a meeting.

3. Practice asking for a favor. You may practice this with neighbors, family, and friends, so it comes naturally to you when you meet a buyer.

4. Imagine you're halfway through a meeting when you

discover that the buyer has misunderstood something important yet basic. You have to address that misunderstanding without making him feel stupid (remember our "no smarty-pants" tip!) and get the sales pitch back on track. Write down how you would do this.

CHAPTER 7

LEARNING BY WATCHING AND DOING

You can't learn how to be an effective salesperson by studying theory from a book, even this book! And I don't think there's a university program offering a degree in "sales." The only way to become a good salesperson is through experience.

Yes, there are courses and workshops that teach useful techniques, and books (like this one) can guide you in the right direction. But this theoretical knowledge is valuable only in combination with practice.

"Practice" means doing it yourself, learning from your own mistakes. It also means observing others, especially those who are already experts in their field to see how they're doing it. It can also mean watching others bungle their attempts, so you see what not to do.

It's like learning a sport. Can you imagine learning how to be a soccer goalie in a classroom, with a teacher writing the correct movements on a whiteboard? You can't become a great soccer goalie or even an adequate one from studying the theory. You need to have tens of thousands of shots aimed at the goal to acquire the skill. You can also refine your own abilities by watching other goalies' mistakes and successes.

FROM MY PERSONAL EXPERIENCE

When I took over my grandmother's cabin business, I had already been her apprentice for ten years. I'd watched and listened to Muffin and my parents, who helped her on the weekends, and come to conclusions. Sometimes, I'd recognize that her way was the best way to do something, and I absorbed it. Other times, I thought, *I could do that better.* So, when my time came, I hit the ground running.

Here are some examples of what I observed:

Muffin used to wait for customers to get out of the car, and then she'd talk to them through the screen door. For her, this made sense. It was convenient, saved time, didn't put a strain on her aging joints, and kept her safe in case the strangers had arrived with harmful intent.

But she lost business this way. Some people would just drive in, look around, and drive back out. Muffin never got the chance to make a sale.

When my parents were helping on weekends, they chose a more proactive approach: They stepped out to greet the customers – and they made more sales. So, I noted the strategy.

I also learned the value of transparency. Sometimes, people rented a cabin. Then they moved in but, an hour later, said, "I changed my mind; this isn't what we wanted." Muffin had to refund their money and reclean the cabin before we could rent it out to someone else. A couple of these instances were enough for me to see the problem. When my turn came, I insisted that customers viewed the cabin before they rented. This way, if it wasn't what they wanted, we didn't have to deal with refunds and extra cleaning work.

On Saturdays, many customers drove up to our cabins to look. Some rented with us, but many others were driving from place to place to compare which one suited them best. In rainy weather, each visitor left dirty footprints and pine needles on the clean floors, which we had to sweep up before the next people arrived to view.

My father hit on the solution: "Let's just close up and wait till people really want to rent, not just look around." When we opened in the late afternoon, we got no more time-wasting "shoppers." By 4pm, people really wanted a place to stay the night – and ours were the last cabins left on the strip. People who drove up were ready to rent.

My father's method worked. It taught me the difference between buyers who merely shop and buyers who are ready to buy, and how to focus my efforts on the latter.

When I initially worked with Philo Smith, he invited me to simply sit in his office while he spoke with people on the phone. These weren't sales conversations as such, but I could hear how professional investors spoke with each other. Every industry has its own language and conversation styles, and he was allowing me to learn the language of professional investors.

My apprenticeship with Art Gartland was intense and fruitful. Art taught me how to underwrite private equity managers and then write all the marketing material. That's how I learned most of what I've shared with you in Chapter 2, "Understand Your Product." When you know the product inside out, you're an effective salesperson who can add real value.

Art took me to client meetings to show me how those unfolded. Each one was different with different investors and priorities. Art taught me how to coach our fund manager clients before and after a meeting with an investor: "This is what's important to this investor, so talk about this more." "Don't act defensive when people push back at you."

CORE INSIGHTS TO TAKE AWAY

- Selling is an apprenticeship. You learn by watching and doing.

- Every industry or market has its own language. Learn yours.

- Listen to and learn from the experienced people around you. Stick with the winners.

- Identify what works for you. Adapt and use it.

- Your apprenticeship begins today and will last your whole life.

- When you read books like this, you're absorbing the authors' experience.

- Watch and listen to your colleagues. What's working and what doesn't work? What would you do differently? Better?

WHAT NOT TO DO

When you have some success, don't think you know it all or have figured it all out. There's always something more to learn from other people.

PROFESSIONAL TIP

Volunteer to be a bag carrier. Do whatever it takes to join a successful colleague at a sales meeting. Carry her bags, set up the computer presentation, get the coffee. Set your ego aside when it comes to learning. Just be there, watch, and learn.

ACTION STEPS

1. Approach your next sales conversation (or your first-ever one) as a practical lesson. Regardless of whether it leads to a sale, you need to learn something from it. At the end, identify at least one thing you can improve upon next time.

2. Find a way to observe an experienced salesperson, preferably in your industry or company. Ask if you

may participate in one of his sales meetings or listen to him making phone calls. Then watch, listen, and learn.

3. Think back to your own sales experiences. Perhaps you've never been a salesperson in a career context – but you may have helped at a charity bazaar, sold your lawn-mowing services for pocket money, or traded baseball cards. What worked? What didn't work? What mistakes did you make? What would you do differently now? Think of at least one lesson you've learned.

CHAPTER 8

HOW TO BE YOUR OWN SUPPORT SYSTEM

Here's a quick story from a friend: At a high-stakes pitch meeting, one of the salespeople was under so much pressure that he couldn't speak when it was his turn. He just froze.

Fortunately, his colleagues took over and covered for him.

Sales is a high-pressure field. There will be moments when you'll be under a lot of pressure. How can you cope?

The demands can be enormous. You need to make calls, research information, attend meetings, provide buyers with information, follow-up on meetings, write sales reports, answer to your superiors, assist colleagues who need help... and all the time, there's the question looming: "When are you going to close this sale?"

And that's just the stress you'll experience in your day-to-day work. Your personal life will throw further challenges at you, as you deal with the demands from your spouse, kids, aging parents, pets, volunteer organization, community, church, or PTA.

People inside and outside of your organization will be rude and make unreasonable demands. As a salesperson hammering out a deal, you're sometimes the negotiator between the world outside your firm and the world inside your firm, and the news you have to deliver may not be what either side wants to hear.

The most stressful factor is that you need to make sales, or you'll experience neither success nor earn a commission or bonus. You'll get a lot of "No's" before you get a "Yes," and that can be disheartening, even terrifying.

When you close on a big sale, you experience the elation of success. The confidence boost, the commission earned, the confirmation that you can really do it, the sheer feeling of achievement, and your sales manager's appreciation act like energizing fuel.

For a short time, you're the hero: appreciated, praised, admired, perhaps even envied… and then it's back to the grind.

Expect lots of hard work, punctuated by the lows of losses and the highs of victories. Anticipating this will help you take it in your stride.

In this chapter, I'll share strategies that work for me. I've learned them through trial and error. You may copy them if you feel any are right for you. Try them out, and adapt them to your personal situation, or use them as inspiration to find your own methods.

TAKE CARE OF YOURSELF

First, you have to take care of yourself. No one else will. Sure, your spouse will probably care for you when you get sick, and your employers may show concern when you're ailing. But you are your own responsibility. You're in charge of your body, your mind, your emotions, your choices.

You must be a friend to yourself.

What does a good friend do? A good friend...

- is emotionally supportive.

- helps you when you need help   whether you ask for the help or not.

- forgives your mistakes.

- calls you out on your crap when you go off the rails.

- loves and has empathy for you despite your shortcomings.

- is honest with you, even when the truth is uncomfortable.

And more.

I'm sure you get the idea: you need to be both demanding *and* forgiving of yourself.

Remember: nobody is perfect. Nobody. They may appear that way in a Hollywood film or on Instagram, but that's just an artificially created image they want you to see. Don't compare yourself against these fake perfections.

Every person you meet has fears and makes mistakes. In fact, those who are best at what they do are often the ones who have made the most mistakes, but they are self-aware and have learned from them.

You'll make mistakes too. That's okay. What matters is that you learn from them.

START EVERY DAY WITH THE COMMITMENT TO DO YOUR BEST

The best way to start your working day is to make a commitment to yourself to do your best. It's as simple as that.

Some days, your "best" will be phenomenal because you feel great and can challenge yourself to high achievements such as saving the company with a once-in-a-lifetime sale. Other days, you'll have a tough time, and doing your best means simply getting out of bed and making it to work. Many days will be somewhere between those extremes.

Whatever your "best" is on any given day, commit to doing it.

WEAR A UNIFORM

Yes, a uniform. But you get to decide what it is.

I went to a parochial school where students had to wear a uniform. a gray sports jacket with a white shirt, the school tie, gray or black trousers, and brown or black dress shoes. Of course, I hated having to wear it – yet, I realized later that it had benefits.

When I wore that uniform, I became a member of that community, a student with the task to learn what I was taught that day. It helped get me in a certain frame of mind. It also saved me the time and mental energy to think about what to wear and to prepare for the day.

As a salesman, I choose to wear a "uniform." It may not look like a uniform to you, but, in my mind, it serves as one.

I have three blue suits on rotation. I chose blue because it's my color. It suits me, and I feel good wearing it. Most of my dress shirts are white, while my ties are blue or purple. I wear black shoes and a black belt.

In this uniform, I look good but not flashy. I don't have to waste time thinking about what to wear. I know that I'm dressed appropriately for meeting potential clients and investors.

In my circles, the conservative look with suit and tie is a sign of respect. For you, a suit may not be the right choice. Depending on the type of people you meet, the situations and locations, a suit might make you appear old-fashioned and overdressed, or worse, unapproachable, arrogant, and out of touch with the buyer's world.

One of my friends aims to dress slightly more formal than his customers, which is a great rule.

Give some thought to what kind of "uniform" your prospective customers would like to see you in.

Even if you're working from home, using the phone rather than meeting buyers in person, take some time and put yourself together. Dress to put yourself in "work mode." This establishes a boundary where you mentally transition from home life to work life. It will come through in how you speak on the phone. You'll sound more professional if you're wearing your "uniform" than if you're slouching in your pajamas.

When I put on my suit in the morning, I mentally slip into the role of professional salesman. This is an immense help.

Another suggestion is to prepare the next day's outfit the night before. Not only does this save time in the morning – especially if you've delayed getting up to the last possible minute – but it prepares your mind.

One of my rugby teams had a tradition of polishing our cleats the night before a game. Ostensibly, it made us look good when we ran out on the field. But one day one of the coaches admitted to me the real reason: polishing our cleats the night before a game got us subconsciously focused on the next day's game.

CREATE A SUPPORT NETWORK

You'll need people on whom you can lean when times are tough.

Fellow salespeople and others with a sales background outside of your organization are ideal.

Friends and family who love you will give you a listening ear and kind words, but they won't really understand the problems. People working for your organization understand a lot, but you'd better not vent to them about what a jerk the sales manager is! Also, they have their own baggage, and you don't need that.

Try to find two or more people who are in sales but outside your organization. Arrange to meet with them regularly or irregularly, whatever suits you all best. Ask them for advice, feedback, fresh perspectives, or simply a listening ear when you vent your frustrations. And importantly, offer the same kind of support when they need it.

If they're friends, you can also meet up spontaneously to talk about acute issues.

Maybe your location or schedule prevent face-to-face meetings. In this case, consider joining an online group. This facilitates the exchange of fresh perspectives, and you can post whenever it's convenient for you. Just be careful not to post anything confidential in a public forum.

In addition, perhaps you can secure the mentorship of an experienced salesperson within your company and benefit from her wisdom. However, be careful not to voice any criticism about the organization, the management, or the product that you don't want to reach your boss.

Several of my closest friends are entrepreneurs, and entrepreneurs are typically involved in sales. I'm part of Entrepreneurs Organization in New York where I have a group of six other entrepreneurs – all salesmen for their firms – with whom I meet monthly to share experiences and challenges.

Find a group of people outside of your company on whom you can lean on when times are tough. Try to talk with them regularly. They don't have to be your best friends, but they have to be available to share similar experiences. Share your experiences and help them if you can. Try not to be judgmental. Sharing what you've experienced is the best way to pass your knowledge on.

AVOID ALCOHOL AND DRUGS

For me, alcohol is a distraction, and I don't need distractions. I don't want to wake up late with a hangover. Alcohol also impairs the judgment. I don't want to say something stupid at a business dinner because I had one too many.

True story: A team of two were on a cross-country flight for a pitch meeting. It had been a long week, and they both had a bit too much to drink. At mealtime, they threw pieces of bread across the cabin at each other, to the consternation of the other passengers in first class. At their meeting the next morning, the bread throwers found that they were pitching to the people who had sat behind them on the flight.

Your stance may be less rigid than mine but be careful. Set yourself a limit and stick with it. I recommend to people who work for me that they don't exceed two drinks at company events.

These days, it's easy to decline a drink. Simply say, "Thanks, I don't drink alcohol," "Thanks, but I'm driving," or "Thanks, I've had enough."

Twenty years ago, this was more of an issue. When turning down a drink, I got funny looks and had to explain myself. Nowadays, people accept this choice.

In some fields, the sales culture involves substance abuse. Salespeople are expected to get drunk or to take mind-altering substances. If you're confronted with such a situation, you need to think about the long-term consequences and make a personal decision whether this is right for you and your health.

NOURISHMENT FOR YOUR MIND

Seek inspiration to become not just better at sales, but better as a person. "A better person" means stronger, kinder, wiser, more balanced, and more serene.

Feed your mind and soul, so they'll grow strong.

I'm not going to prescribe what kind of inspiration you should seek from what sources. Try different options and see what works for you. You can turn to books, listen to sermons, attend lectures, read blogs, or join a philosophy club.

At the end of this guide, I've compiled a list of books I recommend for your inspiration. Take a look.

For me, mental nourishment comes from studying the works of the stoic philosophers. They've helped keep me in perspective as I relate to the world around me. I've subscribed to the "Daily Stoic" email list, so I receive an inspiring quote or thought in my inbox every day.

PERSONAL BOUNDARIES

We live in an era where there has been a severe degradation in people's private lives. It's okay to keep a part of your life for yourself and away from work and online social networks.

It's also okay to let a coworker or buyer know what those boundaries are. If someone is about to cross a boundary or has crossed it, be courteous but clear and firm.

CHOOSE YOUR PASSIVE ENTERTAINMENT CAREFULLY

When I was younger, I spent many hours watching movies and TV. Now I watch a lot less because time is my most valuable asset, and I don't want to give it away to Hollywood. I stopped my cable subscription in 2008.

I don't watch cable news anymore. Listening to people arguing all the time makes me angry and anxious, and those feelings don't help me live a serene, productive life. I'm not trying to deny the world's problems, but I want to protect myself from the negative emotions these news programs try to provoke in me. If I want news, I read it from a wide variety of sources so I can be deliberate about what I want to absorb.

I don't like watching movies that make me anxious or depressed because those emotions then spill over into my life. Instead, I choose to watch mostly sports and comedies. This is what I need to keep my mind balanced and positive.

You may make different choices for your passive entertainment. However, it's important that you choose consciously. Observe what effect different types of entertainment have on your mood, emotions, and energy levels, and select and exclude them accordingly.

EXERCISE

The human body needs physical exercise. It's your responsibility to provide it.

Sometimes, that's a challenge because you may not have the time, resources, or fitness level you need to practice a sport. Simply do whatever you can.

Choose something you enjoy (or at least, don't hate) that fits into your schedule and suits your physical ability, as part of a team or on your own, in regular class-based sessions or whenever you have a few minutes to spare.

You may love taking the tough knocks in competitive karate, or you may prefer the soft energy flow of qi gong. Perhaps playing as part on a team is what motivates you, or maybe you'd rather exercise on your own. Maybe a structured, teacher-led class is right for you, but you could also choose to learn from a DVD. Some find the gym atmosphere motivating, others prefer the privacy of their backyard. Do you like to work out indoors or outside in the fresh air? Are you fit enough to participate in thrilling extreme sports, or is gentle chair yoga all you can manage? Whatever you choose, just do it, even if it's nothing more than lunchtime walks in the local park.

Even a little is better than nothing. The ten-minute exercise you actually do is more beneficial than the one-hour workout you mean to do but keep postponing.

I grew up playing sports, and it was a big part of my identity. Now as a mature adult, I struggle to exercise consistently because I travel a lot for my work, and this disrupts any established routine. A couple of old rugby-related injuries limit what I can physically do. Finding something that fits into my irregular schedule and that I enjoy is a challenge. For example, I've tried both going to the gym and long-distance running and found that neither appeals to me.

Over the years, I've switched between different kinds of exercises, depending on my interest, fitness level, and schedule, even depending on the weather: Some (like rugby, softball, and skeleton racing) I pursued passionately for years, some (like Krav Maga) I practice occasionally, and others (Tae Quon Do, gym, long-distance running) I tried and gave up because I was bored. I do mostly touch rugby, swimming, and Pilates now.

I've been successful in periods when I did a lot of exercise and in times when I did very little. However, I always feel a lot better about myself when I work out.

EAT HEALTHILY

Try to eat healthy meals, even when you're on the road. It can be tempting to just eat junk food for a quick snack, but, in the long run, this isn't going to help your health. Also, be aware that immediately after a meal – especially a fat-laden one – your brain will operate sluggishly while your stomach digests. This can lower the quality of your presentation and slow your thought processes just when you need to be most alert.

SET GOALS

Set goals for yourself. Write them down to make a formal commitment. If possible, share them with someone supportive, so they can ask about your progress. This makes you accountable.

I find that writing the goals down and holding myself accountable to someone really helps. Otherwise, it's easy to think of new goals and to forget them fast.

Setting goals is useful not just for your sales career but also for your personal life, your spiritual development, your training, and more. However, if you're new to working with goals, set just one at a time. Otherwise, having many goals can dilute your focus, and you'll end up not seriously pursuing any.

Keep the goals realistic. Choose targets you know you can achieve, even if the circumstances are not ideal. Life is going to throw challenging obstacles into your way. When you're new to goal-setting, err on the side of the achievable, picking a goal that's too easy rather than one that's difficult to attain. Don't confuse a hope "I hope I can do this" with a practical goal "I will achieve this."

Once you have practice in working with goals and are confident in your abilities, you can stretch yourself and set more challenging goals.

It also helps to focus on goals that are mostly in your control. For example, "Today, I'll make twenty phone calls to prospects" is within your control. "Today, I'll make twenty sales" isn't, because the customers decide whether or not to buy. At the beginning of your sales career, it's wise to stick to goals that are mostly within your control.

Your goals should be realistic. Even if they're outside your comfort zone, they shouldn't be in LaLa Land. Be honest with yourself: what can you really do?

On the other hand, you can allow yourself "crazy" goals too, but only one at a time. I once set myself the goal to master skeleton racing – a sport where you go down an ice track on a sled at 60mph headfirst. At the age of 42, this was a fairly unrealistic goal. Some called it crazy. But I attained a level where I could compete, and it was thrilling!

Set a time for when you'll achieve each goal. Commit to that deadline. I like to break my goals into three types, depending on their duration:

- Short-term goals. These typically span one to three months. Example: "I'm going to connect with ten new investors next month."

- Medium-term goals. These are what I work to achieve in one year. Example: "I'm going to book $1 million in revenue this coming year."

- Long-term goals: For me, they cover three to five years. Example: "I'm going to buy a new apartment."

Notice how these goals are layered. One leads to and builds towards another. If you set one big long-term goal (buying the apartment), you can work backward on how to get there through a series of smaller medium- and short-term goals.

KNOW YOUR ETHICAL STANDARDS AND STICK TO THEM

What are your ethical standards? What matters to you? What would you never do because you think it's wrong? What upsets you when other people do this?

I hope you have clear ethical standards, because you'll need them when you get into sales. Everyone has different values, and that's okay. But you need to know what yours are. For example, your values might include compassion, honesty, generosity, tolerance, or courtesy.

Some unscrupulous salespeople will sell anything to anyone if it makes them money. They'll sell products the customer doesn't need or can't afford, that are faulty, cause long-term harm, or can't do what the salesperson claims. In the short term, some of these people are often phenomenally successful – and brag about it – but their success is often short-lived.

If you haven't thought about this yet, start now. It will make decisions easier when you're confronted with these situations – and you will be confronted.

Some ethical standards have probably been set for you – by your family, your country's laws, your religion's tenets, your company's rules. Adhere by them.

You need to stick to these standards even in the face of temptation and pressure – even if it would mean easy money, even if your own financial situation is desperate, even if the sales manager is breathing down your neck.

Acting against your values will compromise your inner strength and motivation. Think about our section earlier about being a friend to yourself and whether your actions compromise this.

Define your ethical standards. Consider what dilemmas might arise in your line of work, and how you would respond. This way, if you encounter a difficult situation, you'll be ready to make the right decision.

AN ETHICS MISTAKE I MADE AND LEARNED FROM

One summer at our cabin business in New Hampshire, the bat population exploded. Bats may look cute, but they carry diseases like rabies.

The bats got into our house either through a break in a screen door or an open window. I became skilled at capturing the creatures alive in paper bags and releasing them outside.

Sometimes, the bats would get into the cabins, too. One evening that summer, a couple and their young son – who was about nine – drove up our driveway. We had a pleasant conversation walking up the hill to the cabin. Two of our available cabins were suitable for a family of three, and I decided to show the nicer one.

Because it was night, I asked them to wait outside a moment while walked into the cabin and turned on the pull-string light in the middle of the main room. As soon as I walked in, I heard a bat fly past my head. I tried to grab it quickly. I don't know what I would have done if I had randomly caught it because I didn't have a paper bag handy. It was just my first stupid move of many.

I turned the light on and the bat stopped flying. I decided

to hide the problem. If I could just get them to say "Yes," then while Sarah registered the customers, I would quickly run back to the cabin with a paper bag and get the bat out. Hopefully, the bat would never return, and the customers would never find out there had been a problem.

It almost worked. The boy and father came in and liked the cabin. The father actually said, "Yes," but as they were walking out, the bat started flying around again.

"What was that?" the father asked.

I lied. "Um, I think it's a bird. I'll get it out; don't worry."

The boy wasn't fooled. "It's a bat!" he shouted, running out and down the hill to his family's car.

Desperately, I tried to save the sale. "I have another cabin…"

"No, we're leaving!" the father said with so much disdain in his voice that I cringed with shame.

I felt awful afterward for several reasons. The boy was upset, the father was angry, and it was my fault. It was wrong to even let them enter a cabin with a bat in it, let alone rent it to them. Even if I managed to capture the bat and get it out, there would have been no way to keep it out. It had found its way in once and could simply return. (The next day, I discovered the hole in the edge of the window screen where the bat had snuck in and fixed it.)

The moment they left I knew what I should have done: As

soon as I walked into the dark cabin and heard the bat, I should have closed the door, confessed the problem, and taken the customers to the other cabin. If they said no on the spot because they didn't like the inferior cabin or because the thought of bats in the vicinity freaked them out, so be it.

But I was nineteen and wanted to win more than I wanted to do the right thing. I tried to hide the problem and lied…. That lost sale wasn't the bat's fault but mine. I had forfeited the customers' trust. On top of losing a sale, I had compromised my values, and that felt bad.

In your career, you may be faced with the temptation of selling the equivalent of a cabin with a bat in it. Don't do it!

YOU HAD A BAD DAY

Nothing went your way today. Your boss was a jerk. No one wants to talk to you, let alone buy something from you. The big sale you counted on closing today fell through. Even worse, the buyers went with a competitor.

These days have happened to all of us. Don't feel sorry for yourself because self-pity isn't attractive.

Get out of your office. Even if it's your home office.

Do something completely different.

Get some exercise. Go for a walk or to the gym.

Get out of your head. Try to help someone else. Even if it's holding the door open for people at the supermarket. These little things will help you feel better about your day and about yourself.

Tomorrow is a new day. How do you start that day? Start with small victories. Make *one* good call. Have *one* good meeting. Then another. Small victories lead to big victories.

CORE INSIGHTS TO TAKE AWAY

- Be your own best friend.

- Your wellbeing is your responsibility. Take it seriously.

- Create a support network of understanding sales professionals.

- Commit yourself every day to do your best – whatever your best may be on that day.

- Practice some kind of physical workout. Whatever type of exercise suits you is the best for you.

- Choose your passive entertainment (TV, movies) so it doesn't sap your time or emotional energy.

- Set goals. Start with few and modest goals, then work up to stretching yourself.

- Define your ethical standards and abide by them.

- Small victories lead to big victories.

WHAT NOT TO DO

- If you can't cope well with pressure – some people can't – then don't work in sales. Choose a different career.

- Don't be hard on yourself and beat yourself up for failures or mistakes. (View them as learning experiences.)

- Don't set too many goals at once, or unrealistic ones.

- Don't neglect or abuse your body.

- Don't act against your ethical values.

PROFESSIONAL TIP

Make taking care of yourself a priority. This will make it easier to deal with the rest of life's challenges.

FOOD FOR THOUGHT

Here are two of my favorite quotes from Stoic philosophers. Can you see how they apply to being your own support system? Do you agree with them? Wholly? Partially? Why? Why not?

"Some things are in our control and others not. Things in our control are opinion, pursuit, desire, aversion, and, in a word, whatever are our own actions. Things not in our control are body, property, reputation, command, and, in a word, whatever are not our own actions." ~ Epictetus

"He who is a friend to himself is a friend to all mankind." ~ Seneca

ACTION STEPS

In this section, I have several assignments for you. You can spread them out over several days.

1. What's your "uniform" – the kind of clothes that will look great on you and create the right impression in a sales situation? Do you already have it in your wardrobe? If yes, wear it to work. If you don't have the right outfit yet, plan to buy it.

2. Soon after waking up tomorrow, commit to giving your best for that day.

3. Find at least one person who can provide support when you need it, ideally another sales professional who doesn't work for the same company. Approach them and set up a first meeting. Or join an existing support network for salespeople – a local group or an online forum.

4. Be honest with yourself: are you getting enough physical exercise? If not, find a way to incorporate workouts into your daily life. Choose an activity that suits your interest, capabilities, and lifestyle. Commit to at least trying it out.

5. Set yourself a short-term goal. Choose something realistic, achievable, and largely within your control.

If you're new to sales or inexperienced at goal-setting, err on the side of caution and make it too easy rather than too difficult. Set a timeframe by when you'll have achieved this. Write it down and share it with at least one other supportive person.

6. Define your ethical values. What really matters to you? Decide to make this your ethical standard and don't act against it, however strong the pressure or temptation.

CHAPTER 9

DEALING WITH DIFFICULT PEOPLE AND SITUATIONS

Most people are pleasant and professional – but some are not. Here's a quick story:

An investor was giving a private equity manager a hard time at a meeting. Some of it felt personal to the manager. The manager was able to stay calm during the sales meeting but exploded in anger afterward. "I'm never taking a dime from that jerk!"

It turned out that the investor was just testing how the private equity manager acted under pressure and wrote a big check a month later. The manager took the money.

Some situations are just unexpectedly awkward. Another quick story:

Two salespeople walked into a pitch meeting with a group of three buyers. One of them realized that he knew one of the buyers from college. They had had a one-night stand twenty years before and he had never called her back. She remembered him, too.

Prepare yourself for the tricky situations you may encounter, so that when they happen, you'll know how to respond.

Here are some scenarios, and what to do:

WHAT IF THE BUYER DOESN'T TURN UP?

You've arrived punctually for the appointment – but the buyer isn't there. Perhaps a receptionist or assistant tells you, "She'll be with you soon" or "Sorry, she's in a meeting." Or perhaps the buyer phones, and apologizes, "Sorry, I got held up. I'm on my way."

Remind them of the appointment. Ask when the buyer will arrive and request a commitment. If the buyer says, for example, that she's been held up in the traffic but will be there in half an hour, say, "Okay. I'll see you at twelve then."

If the delay is substantial, and you can't stay that long, say so. "Sorry, I have another appointment this afternoon. When can we reschedule?"

If the buyer has put you off more than once, if you feel that she is disrespecting your time (by not attending a meeting although she had committed to the appointment), or if you feel that she simply doesn't want to see you and is fobbing you off with excuses, you may decide not to waste further time with these people.

Sometimes, you'll arrive at an appointment, and the person

you're supposed to meet has forgotten about it and isn't there. Perhaps she's on vacation or at home. In this case, ask if you can see someone else – perhaps her deputy, another team member, her personal assistant, or the head of another department – to make your presentation. These people may not have the power to decide, but they'll have the influence to win the buyer's interest. Show your appreciation that these people are giving you their time at short notice and keep the meeting short and the information simple.

WHAT IF THE BUYER IS UNPLEASANT?

You may choose to put up with a buyer who treats you with aggression or contempt, but you don't have to. Give yourself permission to simply end the conversation and walk away.

When confronted with rudeness, first ask yourself what's going on: Is this person rude to everyone or just you? Is the hostility directed against your company, the product? Is there some history here you don't know about? Or is he simply having a bad day?

Maybe he isn't interested in a purchase but invites salespeople purely so he has someone he can bully. (That's easy: just leave. He's not a qualified buyer.)

It's also possible that he wants to test how you respond to pressure, especially if you'll be involved in the post-sale stage of the project.

Once you've identified why he's behaving badly, you can decide if you want to put up with it. Perhaps you're willing to overlook his rudeness to get the sale, but you may also decide to just walk away.

Remember, money isn't everything. We had a whole chapter on how to take care of yourself. If this character is eating away at your emotional balance or self-worth, then move on. Having a thick skin and an open mind is important in sales, but some people just cannot be tolerated.

If you're fermenting with fury, remove yourself from the situation for long enough to take some calming breaths. Asking for a bathroom break is a good strategy. You can also say that you need to consult with your manager or your company's engineer.

If the buyer's behavior indicates that he wouldn't buy from you (or anyone of your gender, age, ethnicity, etc.) anyway, then there's no point in staying.

Important: If you feel unsafe – because of the buyer's actions, because you feel vulnerable, or even because you simply have a vague gut feeling that something's wrong – don't hesitate. Leave the situation at once.

WHAT IF THE BUYER DOESN'T PAY ATTENTION?

Perhaps the buyer barely listens to what you say, and instead taps text messages or browses the web while you talk.

This can mean that they're simply not interested in the product – or that your presentation is boring. Perhaps she already knows everything you're talking about.

Ask: "What would you like to know about the product?" Then talk about the issues she raises.

If she doesn't raise questions, ask, "Perhaps this isn't a good time to talk about the product?" Although she scheduled this meeting, it's possible that an unrelated issue is preying on her mind and distracting her. She may apologize and confess that a personal emergency is taking up her attention. Perhaps her mother is in the hospital, the surgeons are operating at this moment, and she's anxiously waiting for news. In this case, offer to reschedule the appointment and express your sincere good wishes. The next time you meet, this buyer will probably want to give you the sale because you were so considerate.

On the other hand, if you have the impression that the buyer isn't interested in the product at all, you're probably right. Maybe she has already decided to buy the competitor's product and is just going through the motions so she can show that she has considered other options.

If you can't rouse her interest at all, don't waste your time. Emphasize your product's benefits, stay courteous, but make the meeting short.

WHAT IF THE BUYER CONFESSES THAT HE CANNOT BUY?

Occasionally, after you've spent a lot of time with a buyer, he'll finally confess that he cannot buy from you. Perhaps he never could; he was just pretending to be someone he was not. Maybe he had the authority but not the budget or the money. This is frustrating but remain professional and move on.

He may have believed that he had the money, but something happened after he began speaking with you, and now he no longer has. His budget may have been cut unexpectedly, or all new purchases were frozen for internal reasons. In this situation, you may have a sale in the future. Stay professional and stay in touch.

WHAT IF THE BUYER EXERTS UNETHICAL PRESSURE?

Buyers sometimes press for concessions while negotiating. "I'll order the machine only if I get an upgraded valve with it." That's okay.

But some may try to bribe or blackmail you personally, suggesting a trade-off. That's definitely not okay.

If in doubt, gain time. Say, "I need to think about this" or "I need to discuss this with our engineering team." Then present the dilemma to your sales manager or the members of your personal support team. Do they think the demand is ethical or not? Once you're no longer face to face with the manipulator, you'll find it easier to assess and reject the proposition.

WHAT IF YOU'VE MADE A MISTAKE?

Perhaps you forgot to bring the documentation you promised. Maybe you discover during the presentation that you've miscalculated, not taking a crucial factor into account.

Or perhaps the information you provided previously was wrong.

Whatever went wrong, it's best to admit it and apologize. Then say how (and by when) you'll rectify the error.

PLOWING THROUGH A ROADBLOCK

Twice in my career I've had a lower-level executive be an active roadblock to a sale that had been given the okay by a senior executive. The company wanted to invest in one of our client's products, the decision was made at a high level, but a low-level person was trying to stall the closing for personal reasons. (They didn't like the deal, they wanted to invest in something they preferred, or reasons we'll never know.)

In both cases, I had exhausted every legitimate avenue to work with the problem person. They simply refused to interact with me. So, I had a clear conscience when I went over their head and forced the issue with their superior. I was super diplomatic when I did that, but these senior executives were smart people and figured out the situation in about one minute. In both cases, they forced their junior to close the transaction almost immediately.

It's a difficult choice. We know from Chapter 3 that a buyer's primary fear is often career risk – and now I was ratting them out to their boss.

One of these low-level managers retired shortly afterward. The other... well, I'll probably never close a sale with that firm again. That's the risk I knowingly took. But I closed that sale.

I don't recommend this lightly. But if you do it, get comfortable with the fact that you may or may not close and that you may never do business with that institution again if that lower-level person is still involved.

WALK AWAY, BUT DON'T BURN YOUR BRIDGES

Allow yourself to walk away from unsavory situations. Whatever bothers you – rudeness, lecherous behavior, insults against your ethnicity, disrespect of your time – allow yourself to leave.

Knowing that you have permission to walk away may actually enable you to stay and continue if you wish. It's like an emotional safety valve.

Always stay courteous. Don't let a buyer provoke you into a yelling match with hurled insults. Keep your temper, even if he loses his.

Walk away but try to do it without burning your bridges. You may meet this buyer again in different circumstances, perhaps when you both work for different companies. Sometimes, a badly behaved buyer will even realize what a jerk he was, feel ashamed, and appreciate how you handled the situation. Or you may have dealings with another buyer in the same company. Even if you choose not to pursue the current sale, keep the way open for possible future transactions.

THE BEST WAY TO FIND SOLUTIONS

Once you've removed yourself from a difficult situation or dilemma, go for a walk or jog. This works off the frustration and clears your mind. After a short while – probably after around twenty minutes – you'll see more clearly. Creative thoughts will come flowing in. With this fresh perspective and new ideas, you'll be able to map out a new plan of action.

CORE INSIGHTS

- Whatever happens, remain professional.

- You don't need to tolerate bad behavior. You decide what you're willing to put up with. Allow yourself to walk away if a buyer transgresses your boundaries.

- Try to find out what motivates the buyer's behavior and base your decision on this.

- If unsure how to react, buy yourself time to think.

PROFESSIONAL TIP

If you get the impression that a buyer's poor or inconsistent behavior is just cover for a "No," move on quickly. Time is your most valuable commodity. Don't waste it.

ACTION STEPS

1. Imagine a scenario where the buyer's behavior is unacceptable – perhaps he's rude, makes inappropriate personal remarks, or hints that he is willing to trade unethical favors.

Think of ways to walk away without burning your bridges. What can you say to bring the meeting to an end fast, yet remain calm and polite?

You may want to practice this in role-play with members of your support team.

2. Imagine that your train or flight is delayed, or that you're stuck in a traffic jam or have lost your way. You hope that you'll still arrive on time, but you can't be certain, so you phone the buyer to say that you may be late. What will you say? How will you say it? Practice that call and record your voice.

3. Imagine you're on time, but the buyer isn't. She phones to say that she's on her way. How will you respond? Decide what to say and record yourself saying it.

A FINAL WORD – AND THE SECRET TO YOUR SUCCESS

Congratulations! You're at the end of the book. By taking the action steps in each chapter, you now have a plan, and a process for surviving and excelling in sales.

Let's recap together:

- You know what you're selling better than anyone.

- You understand the types of buyers you'll pitch to and their motivations.

- You've practiced and are well prepared.

- You know how to get going. You're either not afraid or you've punched through that initial fear with action.

- You have some of my practical tips and have begun to learn from the pros in action through apprenticeship. Soon you'll have your own list because you'll be the pro.

- And, you know how to take care of yourself, which will make you resilient.

And you'll need to be resilient because here is the final word. It's the key to much of the success I've had:

Persistence.

It sounds easy, but it's not. Over time, you'll watch your colleagues in sales drop away from you as they run into challenging streaks and don't know what to do next, or just give up.

They don't have a process and a system to fall back on. You do.

If they have success, they may confuse it with luck, or they have a hot product for a moment in time. Or their firm's brand helps them. So, when times get tough, they won't know what to do.

You will. Go back to the basics. The product, the buyer, take an action, jump over all the hurdles, take away all the "No's" and get to the "Yes" of a close.

It's keeping the store open an extra half hour when everyone else is closed and you want to go home.

It's one more call after everyone's left the office.

It's reading the trade magazine to find another lead instead of watching TV.

Keep trying. You must be persistent. It's simple, but not always easy. Understand that and embrace persistence as one more of your competitive advantages

Have faith in yourself and your system and I wish you the best of success.

Patrick

RECOMMENDED READING

Here are some books with insights and inspirations you may find useful for your sales career. Some offer directly relevant advice; others help you to become ethically strong.

Dale Carnegie: *How to Win Friends & Influence People*
This classic, first published in 1936, is one of the most influential books ever. Its timeless advice will help you win the favor of buyers and establish good relationships in other areas of your life.

Timothy Gallway: *The Inner Game of Tennis*
I love this book and I don't even play tennis! The author describes two aspects of ourselves: the ego/conscious aspect which looks at how we think things are supposed to be/happen and the natural state where we know what to do without consciously thinking about it and are just naturally reacting to what's happening. This is what we want to achieve in our selling.

Ryan Holiday: *Ego is the Enemy*
When you achieve success, you may find that you are your own worst enemy. This book will help you stay grounded.

Ryan Holiday: *The Obstacle is the Way*
Obstacles are opportunities to do something different, to grow and practice courage.

Matthew Michalewicz: *Life in Half a Second*
This is a great book about understanding how short our lives are and setting up a plan for the life you want to lead.

Robert Ringer: *Million Dollar Habits*
A classic recommended to me by my favorite business school professor, Jim Schraeger at the University of Chicago. Some of my colleagues thought the book was corny, but I loved it. Very practical advice about dealing with reality and having the right attitude to enable your success.

John Ruhlin: *Giftology*
John articulates his philosophy as well as successes and failures around gift giving. He tells you what works and what doesn't and why.

Zig Ziglar: *Selling 101*
This short, concise book is useful when you're new to the field. There's also a longer version – *Ziglar on Selling* – but if you want quick, to-the-point advice, the small book is a great start.

ACKNOWLEDGMENTS

I want to thank everyone who helped make my life, my sales career, and this book a success:

My mother and father, Kay and Michael Campbell, gave me a ton of responsibility at a very young age, which has largely shaped who I am in business. From my mother I learned steadiness and persistence. And when it came time to start my own company, I knew what to do without hesitation, because I had watched my father do it most of my life.

Nancy Owens Hess hired me at CET, which I haven't spoken about much in the book, but was the right place at the right time for me. Elvira Hammond convinced me to work at CET when she said to me as an intern struggling about whether I should stay full time, "Why don't you just make a decision to stay here and learn as much as you can." I've kept that advice everywhere I've gone since.

Jim Amen recruited me out of the University of Chicago, and our boss, Philo Smith, gave me my start and mentored me in a career that would lead me to owning my own business.

Similarly, Arthur Gartland hired me at Benedetto, Gartland

& Co. and mentored me and I've tried to retain the good advice he gave me through his words and actions. At BGC, my partner Russell Pennoyer was a great example of polite persistence and demonstrated a work ethic second to none.

When I started my own firm, Perth Advisors, several people were supportive, including former clients Steve Blewitt and Bob McKeon. One of the wonderful things about satisfied buyers is that they sometimes send you referrals. And for that, I'm grateful to Steve Palmer for introducing me to Jay Rollins and Maren Steinberg, who have been an important part of the growth of our company. More than anyone, Jay has shown me how important education is in the marketing process.

I've had some great friends but four have really carried me through good times and bad: Jonathan Hirst, Pete Meyers, Greg Burgess, and Immanuel Thangaraj.

Some other people who have been important in my life include all my grandparents, Muffin, Ollie, and William Griffin; my sister Sarah; John Willy; and teachers David Southworth, Dan Wise, John Ogden, John Pittuck, Freddie Bryan-Brown, Chris Woodhouse, Allen Linden, Janet Polasky, Jerry Grieder, Jim Schraeger and Randy Krozner.

This is a book that I've started to write several times, and Rayne Hall and The Books Factory helped me finally put it all together in a coherent way. In addition, friends, Stanley Meytin, Dominic Piccirillo, John Faxio, Andrew Stein and Eric Horwitz served as beta readers with valuable input based on experience.

Last, but most definitely not least, I thank my wife, Yasmine, who is a fantastic mother and a great wife.

I'm sure I've forgotten someone, so forgive me ahead of time.

Thank you, and I send you all my love and gratitude.

Patrick